Love is patient

Love is kind

Love is not jealous

Love does not brag and is not arrogant

Love does not act unbecomingly

Love does not rejoice in unrighteousness, but rejoices with the truth

Love bears all things, believes all things, hopes all things, endures all things

Love is patient

Love is kind

Love is not jealous

Love does not brag and is not arrogant

Love does not act unbecomingly

Love does not rejoice in unrighteousness, but rejoices with the truth

Love bears all things, believes all things, hopes all things, endures all things

Love never fails

1 Corinthians 13:4–13

Love is patient

Love is kind

Love is not jealous

Love does not brag and is not arrogant

Love does not act unbecomingly

Love does not rejoice in unrighteousness, but rejoices with the truth

Love bears all things, believes all things, hopes all things, endures all things

Love never fails

1 Corinthians 13:4–13

Love is patient

Love is kind

Love is not jealous

Love does not brag and is not arrogant

Love does not act unbecomingly

Love does not rejoice in unrighteousness, but rejoices with the truth

Love bears all things, believes all things, hopes all things, endures all things

Love never fails

1 Corinthians 13:4–13

Love is patient

Love is kind

Love is not jealous

Love does not brag and is not arrogant

Love does not act unbecomingly

*Love does not rejoice in unrighteousness,
but rejoices with the truth*

Love bears all things, believes all things, hopes all things, endures all things

Love never fails

1 Corinthians 13:4–13

Love is patient

Love is kind

Love is not jealous

Love does not brag and is not arrogant

Love does not act unbecomingly

Love does not rejoice in unrighteousness, but rejoices with the truth

Love bears all things, believes all things,
hopes all things, endures all things

Love never fails

1 Corinthians 13:4–13

Love is patient

Love is kind

Love is not jealous

Love does not brag and is not arrogant

Love does not act unbecomingly

Love does not rejoice in unrighteousness,
but rejoices with the truth

*Love bears all things, believes all things,
hopes all things, endures all things*

Love never fails

1 Corinthians 13:4–13

Love is patient

Love is kind

Love is not jealous

Love does not brag and is not arrogant

Love does not act unbecomingly

Love does not rejoice in unrighteousness, but rejoices with the truth

Love bears all things, believes all things, hopes all things, endures all things

Love never fails

1 Corinthians 13:4-13

Love is patient

Love is kind

Love is not jealous

Love does not brag and is not arrogant

Love does not act unbecomingly

*Love does not rejoice in unrighteousness,
but rejoices with the truth*

Love bears all things, believes all things, hopes all things, endures all things

Love never fails

1 Corinthians 13:4–13

Love is patient

Love is kind

Love is not jealous

Love does not brag and is not arrogant

Love does not act unbecomingly

*Love does not rejoice in unrighteousness,
but rejoices with the truth*

Love bears all things, believes all things, hopes all things, endures all things

Love never fails

1 Corinthians 13:4-13

Love is patient

Love is kind

Love is not jealous

Love does not brag and is not arrogant

Love does not act unbecomingly

*Love does not rejoice in unrighteousness,
but rejoices with the truth*

Love bears all things, believes all things, hopes all things, endures all things

Love never fails

1 Corinthians 13:4-13

Love is patient

Love is kind

Love is not jealous

Love does not brag and is not arrogant

Love does not act unbecomingly

Love does not rejoice in unrighteousness, but rejoices with the truth

Love bears all things, believes all things,
hopes all things, endures all things

Love never fails

1 Corinthians 13:4–13